29

Rising Stars UK Ltd.
22 Grafton Street, London W1S 4EX
www.risingstars-uk.com

Helping Everyone Achieve

NASEN House, 4/5 Amber Business Village, Amber Close, Amington,
Tamworth, Staffordshire B77 4RP

Every effort has been made to trace copyright holders and obtain their permission for the use of copyright materials. The publisher will gladly receive information enabling them to rectify any error or omission in subsequent editions.

All facts are correct at time of going to press.

The right of Andy Seed to be identified as the author of this work has been asserted by him in accordance with the Copyright, Design and Patents Act 1988.

Published 2008

Text, design and layout © Rising Stars UK Ltd.
Series Consultant: Lorraine Petersen
Cover design: Neil Straker Creative
Cover photograph: Alamy
Design: Geoff Rayner, Bag of Badgers
Editorial: Frances Ridley
Illustrations: Bill Greenhead for Illustration Ltd.
Photographs:
AKG Images: 13, 18, 41
Alamy: 22, 24, 25
Kobal Collection: 19, 32, 35, 42, 46
Samuel Ralli, photograph: 44-45
Vinmag Archive: 4, 8, 10, 12, 14, 20, 23, 27, 40, 45

British Library Cataloguing in Publication Data.
A CIP record for this book is available from the British Library.

ISBN: 978-1-84680-445-8

Printed by: Craftprint International Ltd, Singapore

CONTENTS

GRAPHIC NOVELS: THE BIG PICTURE   5

ZOOMING IN...   6

SUPERHEROES   9

BEST SELLERS   15

MANGA MANIA   21

CLOSE-UP: WHAT'S ON THE PAGE?   26

SPIN-OFF SPY   31

MORE THAN STORIES   37

A DARK TALE   43

GLOSSARY/INDEX   48

GRAPHIC NOVELS: THE BIG PICTURE

Not all books tell stories in words. Some books use pictures. They're like grown-up comics – and they're exciting to read. Welcome to the world of graphic novels.

FOCUS

FIND OUT THE ANSWERS TO THESE QUESTIONS.

1 WHAT IS STRANGE ABOUT POINT BLANC SCHOOL?

2 DO YOU READ MANGA FROM LEFT TO RIGHT?

3 WHAT MAKES OBELIX SO STRONG?

ZOOMING IN...

V for Vendetta
A dark and scary future.

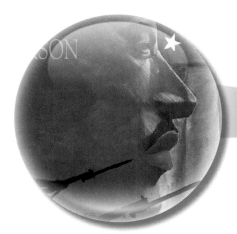

King
A real-life hero.

Alex Rider
You're never too young to die...

The Silver Surfer

With superheroes,
anything can happen.

Fungus
the Bogeyman

Life with slime, boils and goo!

Ghost Hunt

Spooky stuff from Japan.

Manga and Fowl

Learn the language
of comic books.

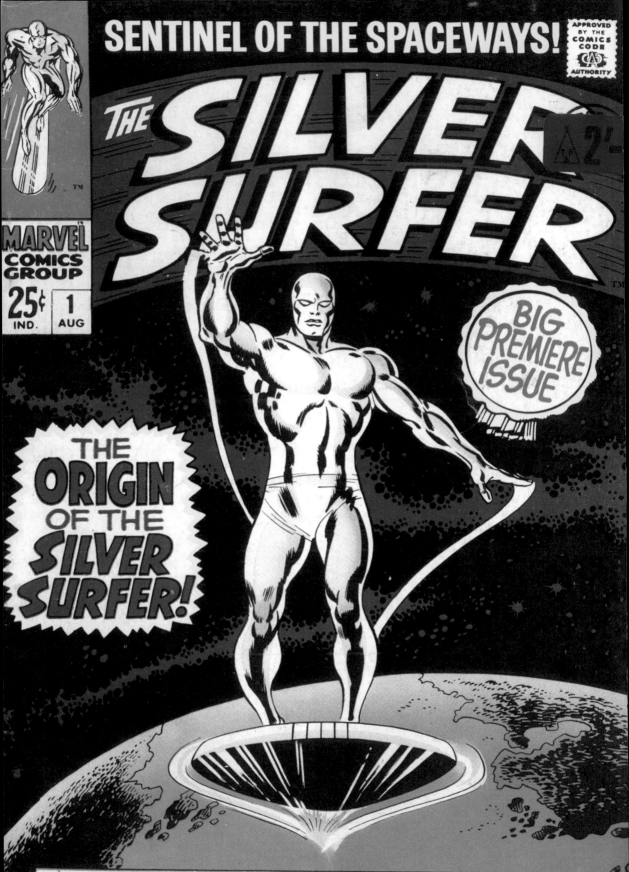

SUPERHEROES

THE SILVER SURFER IS A SUPERHERO. HE FIRST APPEARED IN A COMIC STRIP IN 1966.

THEN HE APPEARED IN A LONGER STORY CALLED THE SILVER SURFER. IT WAS A BOOK, NOT A COMIC. THE GRAPHIC NOVEL WAS BORN.

Welcome to Graphic Novel Review
The website about superhero graphic novels

- Superman
- Batman
- Spider-Man
- Wonder Woman
- The Hulk
- Captain Marvel
- More

THIS WEEK'S STAR HERO

BATMAN

Batman fights crooks and rescues people in trouble.

Great artwork and strong stories! 9/10

Graphic novels in libraries:

- There are lots of GNs in libraries

- Check out your local library for some cool superhero adventures

- Borrowing books is free!

Comics vs Graphic Novels What's the difference?

Comic	Graphic Novel
Shorter – about 32 pages	Longer – mostly over 100 pages
Lots of stories	One story
Paper cover	Card cover
Looks like a magazine	Looks like a book
Mostly about superheroes and funny characters	Sometimes about ordinary people
For younger readers	For older readers

ELEKTRA

Elektra is another superhero. She is an **assassin** who uses two swords called sai. She has been in comics and graphic novels. Elektra first appeared in *Daredevil* comic in 1981. The comic had stories about other characters, too. Later, Elektra had a comic of her own.

Elektra was a popular character with older readers.
She started to appear in graphic novels.
The first one came out in 1990. It was called
Elektra Lives Again.

FUNGUS the BOGEYMAN
RAYMOND BRIGGS

BEST SELLERS

GRAPHIC NOVELS SOON BECAME POPULAR. SOME OF THEM BECAME BEST-SELLERS, LIKE FUNGUS THE BOGEYMAN. FUNGUS'S JOB IS TO SCARE PEOPLE. HE LOVES DIRT AND ANYTHING THAT STINKS.

ASTERIX WAS ANOTHER POPULAR SERIES OF GRAPHIC NOVELS. THE ASTERIX BOOKS CAME FROM FRANCE.

Diary of an Asterix Fan

7th August

First day of my holiday. Today I read my favourite book again, Asterix the Gaul. Asterix lives in a small village in **Ancient Gaul**. He's very strong because he drinks magic **potion**. The best part is when he bashes the Romans.

11th August

Today I read Asterix in Britain. This book is really funny – my dad likes it too. The best part is the rugby match. Obelix is a great character. He's really strong because he fell into the magic potion as a baby.

14th August

I finished Asterix and the Roman Agent today. I love these graphic novels. They are full of jokes, silly names and fantastic drawings. I want to get all 33 books!

R. GOSCINNY · Asterix · A. UDERZO

Asterix
THE GAUL

Written by
René GOSCINNY

Illustrated by
Albert UDERZO

UDERZO 61

WHAT MAKES A BEST SELLER?

Best sellers have strong characters and stories. They are popular with children *and* adults.

GN FACT

FUNGUS, ASTERIX, TINTIN AND THE SNOWMAN HAVE ALL BEEN MADE INTO FILMS, TV CARTOONS AND PLAYS.

Author File:
Hergé

© Hergé/Moulinsart 2008

Country: Belgium

Series: *Tintin*

About: the adventures of a young reporter and his dog Snowy.

Fact: this series of books has sold over 200 million copies in 50 languages.

Author File:
Raymond Briggs

Country: UK

Book: *The Snowman*

About: a Snowman that comes to life.

Fact: the book has no words at all!

GHOST HUNT

Manga by **Shiho Inada**   Story by **Fuyumi Ono**

MANGA MANIA

MANGA ARE COMICS AND GRAPHIC NOVELS FROM JAPAN. THEY ARE VERY POPULAR ALL OVER THE WORLD. THE WORD 'MANGA' MEANS 'CRAZY SKETCHES'. THEY SPREAD FROM JAPAN IN THE 1990S. TV SERIES LIKE POKÉMON WERE BASED ON MANGA.

DON'T MISS MELTON'S MASSIVE

MANGA FAIR

NEW TO MANGA?
THEN COME AND FIND OUT MORE!
SEE THE AMAZING RANGE
OF COMIC BOOKS
FROM JAPAN.

We stock manga for young and old

ALL TYPES OF MANGA FOR SALE!

Action!
Romance!
Drama!
Comedy!
Adventure!
Sports!
Sci-fi!
Fantasy!
Mystery!
Horror!

Top-selling manga in English:

- Dragon Ball

- Fruits Basket

- Naruto

- Death Note

- Love Hina

- Battle Club

- Ghost Hunt

- Pokémon

Hundreds of graphic novels for girls and boys

Weekly and monthly comics
Manga collections

RIGHT TO LEFT

Most manga stories are printed in comics first. Each comic has different series in it. After a while, the stories from one series are put together. They are made into a graphic novel.

PHONE BOOKS

MANGA FACTS

- MOST MANGA ARE WRITTEN FROM RIGHT TO LEFT.

- JAPAN HAS SPECIAL MANGA CAFÉS.

- THE MOST POPULAR MANGA SERIES ARE MADE INTO ANIME. ANIME ARE ANIMATED CARTOONS.

- SOME MANGA BOOKS ARE 850 PAGES LONG THEY ARE CALLED 'PHONE BOOKS'!

- EACH YEAR IN JAPAN, PEOPLE SPEND OVER £2,000,000,000 ON MANGA!

CLOSE UP: WHAT'S ON THE PAGE?

FRAME

SPEECH BUBBLE

MOVEMENT LINES

SMALL PANEL

LARGE PANEL

SYMBOLS AND LARGE LETTERS

CLOSE-UP

ARTEMIS FOWL

EOIN COLFER'S
ARTEMIS FOWL

Adapted by EOIN COLFER and ANDREW DONKIN

THE GRAPHIC NOVEL
Art by GIOVANNI RIGANO Colour by PAOLO LAMANNA

HEADING

DETAILED DRAWING
TO SET THE SCENE

BOLD TEXT

CAPITAL LETTERS

EXTRA LARGE PANEL
TO SHOW SETTING

CAPTION

DUST EFFECT MADE
BY COMPUTER

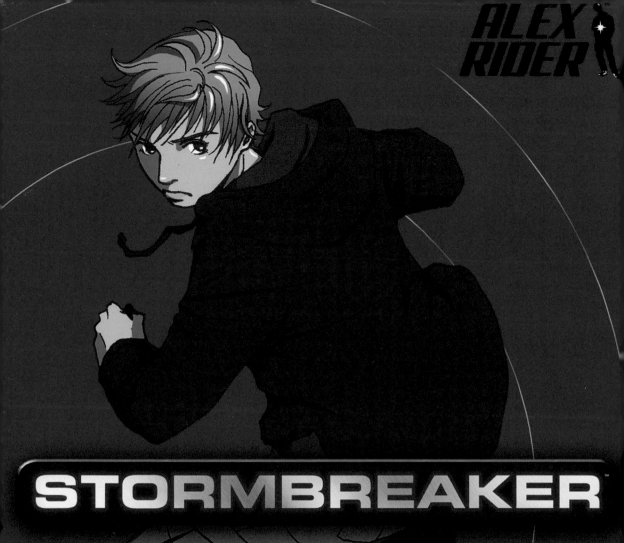

STORMBREAKER

THE GRAPHIC NOVEL

ANTHONY HOROWITZ

Antony Johnston · Kanako and Yuzuru

SPIN-OFF SPY

ALEX RIDER IS A COOL TEENAGE SPY. HE FIRST
APPEARED IN THE NOVEL STORMBREAKER.
THE NOVEL WAS THEN MADE INTO A FILM.

NOW ALEX RIDER IS IN GRAPHIC NOVELS, TOO.
THESE ARE BASED ON THE BOOKS AND FILMS –
THEY ARE 'SPIN-OFFS'.

Dear Matt,

Happy birthday! I hope you have a great day and that you enjoy this book.

It's the graphic novel of Stormbreaker. I've seen the film – it's about a boy called Alex Rider. He finds out that his uncle was a spy. Then he's asked to go on a mission for MI6.

The film had lots of action and **gadgets**, like James Bond.

I may be an uncle but I'm glad I'm not a spy (I don't want to be shot!).

Love from

Uncle Bob

SCARY SCHOOL!

The second Alex Rider novel is called *Point Blanc*.

Point Blanc: the Graphic Novel is about a school which is built on top of a snowy mountain! Alex Rider goes there to solve a mystery.

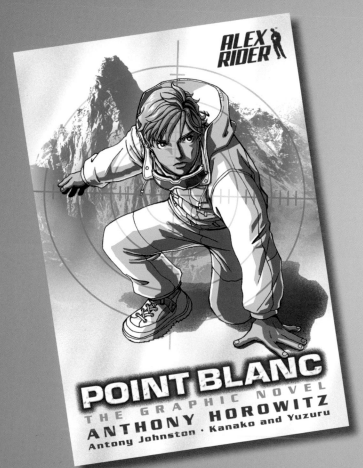

ALEX RIDER

POINT BLANC
THE GRAPHIC NOVEL
ANTHONY HOROWITZ
Antony Johnston · Kanako and Yuzuru

FUN FACT

ALEX RIDER BITES HIS NAILS WHEN HE IS WORRIED. THAT'S NOT SO COOL!

These graphic novels are also based on books, TV and films:

- The Hobbit
- Doctor Who
- Artemis Fowl
- Star Trek
- Heroes

THE TV SHOW HEROES HAS A GRAPHIC NOVEL SPIN OFF

MORE THAN STORIES

MARTIN LUTHER KING WAS A REAL-LIFE HERO. HE LED BLACK PEOPLE IN AMERICA TO FIGHT FOR THEIR RIGHTS. HIS STORY IS TOLD IN PICTURES IN THE GRAPHIC NOVEL KING. THERE ARE THREE VOLUMES OF KING.

King Vol.1 by Ho Che Anderson

Review

By **Sumi Ako** - see my other reviews

This book tells the true story of Martin Luther King. He was a church leader in the USA. In the 1950s and '60s he helped black people to get the same rights as white people.

The book is a **biography** set out like a graphic novel. The comic book style is a great way to tell this story. The pictures are black and white but they are very powerful. They really bring the events to life. You feel you are there with King – making speeches and going on protest marches.

I enjoyed this book. It made me understand how hard life was for black people in America. Read this book if you like graphic novels or history!

 Average Review

Was this review helpful to you? (Yes) (No)

REAL LIFE IN PICTURES

KING tells the real-life story of Martin Luther King. These three graphic novels also tell true stories in pictures.

Maus

ABOUT: The author's father.

STORY: Tells how the **Nazis** made him suffer.

FACT: Some of the characters have mice heads.

Comanche Moon

ABOUT: The last days of the **Comanche** Indians.

STORY: Tells how the Comanches lost their land.

FACT: An exciting history book.

Ethel and Ernest

ABOUT: Raymond Briggs' parents.

STORY: Tells how they survived a war.

FACT: Briggs also wrote *The Snowman*.

A DARK TALE

V FOR VENDETTA IS A FAMOUS GRAPHIC NOVEL BY
ALAN MOORE. IT'S SET IN AN UNHAPPY FUTURE.
A MAN IN A **GUY FAWKES** MASK APPEARS. HE IS
CALLED V AND HE FIGHTS BACK AGAINST THE
EVIL RULERS.

Profile : Alan Moore
Comic Book Legend

Job:
> Writer of comics
> and graphic novels.

Most famous books:
> **V for Vendetta.**
> **Watchmen.**

Comic characters he has worked on:
> Swamp Thing, The Hulk,
> Batman, and many others.

Other writing:
> Novels, poems, short stories
> and a film.

Music:
> Played in a band called
> 'The Sinister Ducks'.

Awards:
> Has won over 20 awards and
> prizes for his comic book writing.

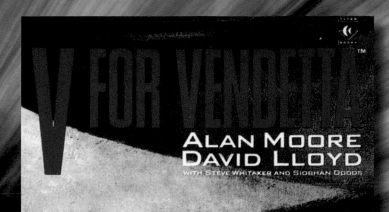

Other facts:

- He started out drawing cartoons.

- He is a **vegetarian.**

- He performs magic.

- He 'appeared' as himself in *The Simpsons* in 2007.

- Many of his stories have been made into films.

NEW DIRECTIONS

The first graphic novels were about superheroes.
They have come a long way since then. *V for Vendetta*
is about real people. There are no monsters or
spaceships in it. *Persepolis* is the true story of a girl
growing up in Iran. It's the author's life story. In 2007
it was made into a film.

The first graphic novels were long comics. Now, they come in different formats. There are special books for collectors. These are printed on expensive paper. And there are graphic novels on the Internet!

GLOSSARY

Ancient	Ancient means very old.
Assassin	Someone hired to kill a another person.
Biography	A person's life story written by another person.
Comanche	Native American Indians, pronounced 'kuh-man-chee'.
Fantasy	Stories about magic and adventure.
Gadget	A small object that does something clever. Alex Rider has zit cream that can eat through steel.
Gaul	The old Roman name for France.
Guy Fawkes	A man who lived about 400 years ago in England. He tried to kill the King by blowing up the Houses of Parliament
Nazi	The Nazi party ruled Germany during World War II. The Nazis were cruel to many groups of people.
Potion	A drink that makes something happen.
Vegetarian	A person who doesn't eat meat.
Vendetta	A fight that goes on for a very long time.

INDEX

Alan Moore	44-45	Martin Luther King	36-39
Alex Rider	30-34	Maus	40
Artemis Fowl	28-29	Raymond Briggs	19, 41
Asterix	15-17	Silver Surfer	9
Elektra	12-13	Tintin	18-19
Fungus the Bogeyman	14-15	*V for Vendetta*	43, 44, 46
Manga	20-27		